meet the family
My
Grandparents

by Mary Auld

W

FRANKLIN WATTS
LONDON•SYDNEY

LINCOLNSHIRE
COUNTY COUNCIL

This is Patrick with his dad's parents – Granny Frances and Grandpa Bill. They are two of Patrick's four grandparents.

This is James with his mum's dad. He calls him Grandad.

Sien and An were
very sad when
their grandpa
died. They like
to remember him
by looking at
photos of him
with their parents.

Rosie's grandmother looks after her when her mum is at work.

Ed's grandparents live with him and the rest of the family.

Ali's grandpa is a doctor.

Claire's grandma
works in a shop.

Pete's grandpa is retired. Now he spends lots of time with Pete. They make all sorts of things together.

Kirstie likes staying the
night at her grandparents.

Mick's grandad takes him swimming.

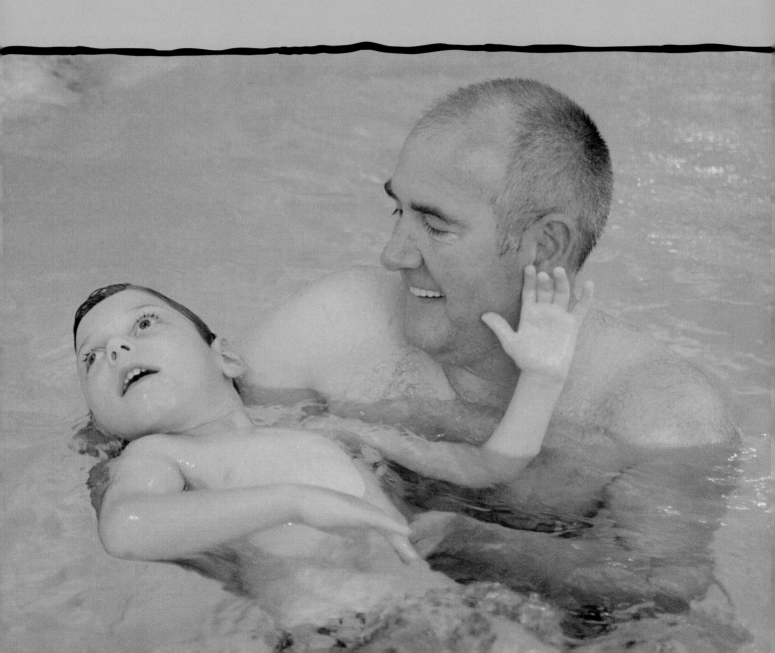

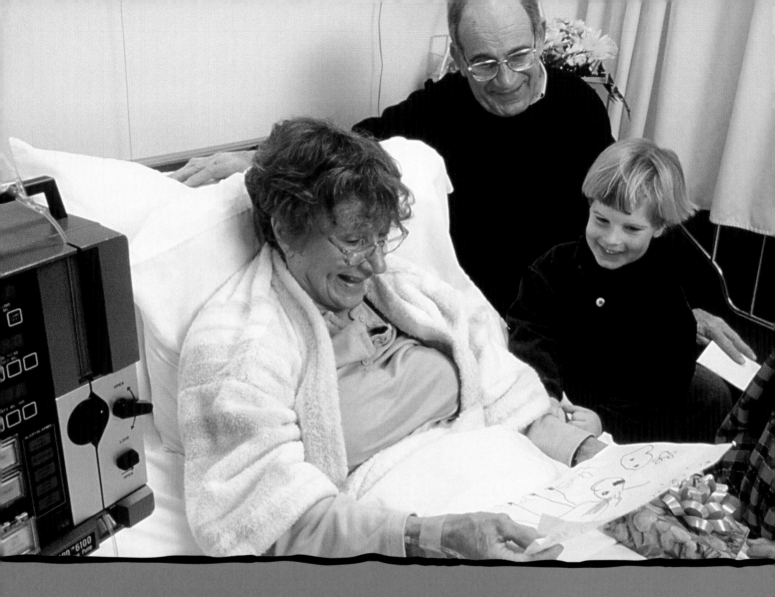

Ben's grandma isn't well.
Ben goes with his grandpa
to visit her in hospital.

Hannah's grandparents live a long way away – in another country. She often talks to them on the phone.

This is Saffron with her mum, her granny and her mum's granny – Saffron's great-granny.

What are your grandparents like?

Family words

Here are some words people use when talking about their grandparents or family.

Names for grandparents:
**Gran, Granny, Grandma, Grandmother;
Grandad, Grandpa, Grandfather.**

Names for parents:
**Father, Daddy, Dad, Pa;
Mother, Mummy, Mum, Ma.**

Names of other relatives:
**Sister, Brother; Daughter, Son;
Uncle; Aunt, Auntie; Nephew; Niece.**

If we put the word 'great' in front of a relative's name it means that they are separated from us by an extra generation of family. Look at the family tree on page 24; each level on it is a generation.

A family tree

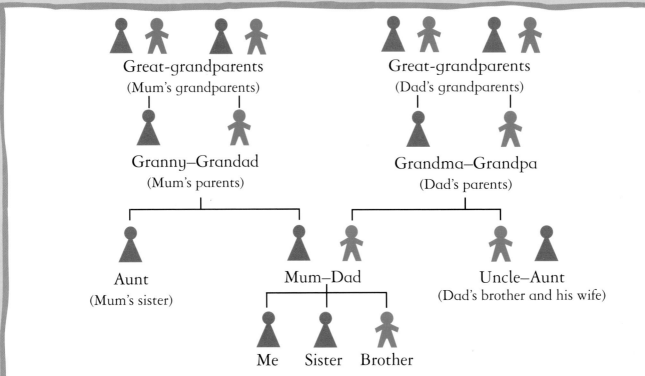

Great-grandparents
(Mum's grandparents)

Great-grandparents
(Dad's grandparents)

Granny–Grandad
(Mum's parents)

Grandma–Grandpa
(Dad's parents)

Aunt
(Mum's sister)

Mum–Dad

Uncle–Aunt
(Dad's brother and his wife)

Me   Sister   Brother

You can show how you are related to all your family
on a plan like this one. It is called a family tree.
Every family tree is different. Try drawing your own.

First published in 2003 by Franklin Watts,
96 Leonard Street, London EC2A 4XD

Franklin Watts Australia
45-51 Huntley Street, Alexandria, NSW 2015

Copyright © Franklin Watts 2003

Series editor: Rachel Cooke
Art director: Jonathan Hair
Design: Andrew Crowson
A CIP catalogue record for this book
is available from the British Library.

ISBN 0 7496 4885 6

Printed in Hong Kong/China

Acknowledgements:
Bruce Berman/Corbis: front cover centre below.
www.johnbirdsall.co.uk: front cover top, 12, 17. Jon
Feingersh/Corbis: 9. Carlos Goldin/Corbis: front
cover main, 22. Sally Greenhill/Sally & Richard
Greenhill PL: 5, 10-11. Tom & Dee Ann McCarthy/
Corbis: 6, 19b. Brian Mitchell/Photofusion: 16. Jose
Luis Pelaez/Corbis: front cover bottom, 19cl. Karen
Robinson/Photofusion: 13. George Shelley/Corbis:

front cover centre above. Ariel Skelley/Corbis: front
cover centre, 20. Liz Somerville/Photofusion: 2. Tom
Stewart/Corbis: 18. David Woods/Corbis: 1, 14-15.

Whilst every attempt has been made to clear
copyright should there be any inadvertent
omission please apply in the first instance to
the publisher regarding rectification.